Staying Near The Water

THOMAS HENRY CARTER

Outskirts Press, Inc.
http://www.outskirtspress.com

Paperback ISBN: 978-1-9772-3952-5
Hardback ISBN: 978-1-9772-2608-2

Outskirts Press and the "OP" logo are trademarks belonging to Outskirts Press, Inc.

PRINTED IN THE UNITED STATES OF AMERICA

Thank you for your inspirations. You know who you are.

"Those who were seen dancing were thought to be insane by those who could not hear the music." - Friedrich Nietzsche.

"Think, it ain't illegal yet"- Eddie Griffin

"I may not change the world but I will ignite the spark who will"- Tupac 'Makaveli' Shakur

Contents

Introduction

About 'Staying Near the Water'

What if gain came at loss of nothing worth keeping? Imagine, food was food, love was love, and time did not mean something good was ending. 'Staying Near the Water' muses a transient value system via haiku, unstamped letter, and freestyle expression.

During a heartfelt conversation, beloved Kenny Tyson once asked, "Hank, you don't have many friends do you?" Thomas smiled and asked why would Kenny ask such? Kenny simply replied, "Because you are honest." 'Morning Glory' was recognized by The Tennessee Magazine Poetry Contest in April 2018.

From the Editor: "Keep this in mind Hank, poetry is difficult. That is why sometimes, you harbor doubts about your ability to adequately express what you are passionately driven to say. Don't worry. ALL poets struggle with that delicate nature that is poetry. Take heart in this: Poetry is also fun. Writing poetry, experimenting with poetic forms, and language construction can be exhilarating. Have fun with tanka and haiku; but never underestimate their value, and worth. And try, when you can, to return to the sense of the natural world which is the true domain of both these poetic forms.

Remember, poetry is not a science; it is an art form and is always open to interpretation. The only way to succeed is to read, write, imagine, and never stop...Remember Son, do not be proud of what you have accomplished, but always respect your work."

Love, Dad

Credits

Editor and Consultant
Larry Roosevelt Carter, MFA

Graphics
Cover- Shyanne Shadelle Williams
Phil W. Gomez

Rosetta Ford October 8, 1926 to February 6, 2017

'Luella's Song' as recited by
Rosetta 'Granny Rose' Ford

I know bluer violets sparkle with dew or morn
I know now where you come from
And the way that you were born
When God cut holes in heaven
The holes that the stars shine through
The little scraps fell down to the earth
And the little scraps are you

'Rosetta's Song' as recited
by our friend Rosetta

They say there is no place like home
And I believe it is true
No other spot in all the world
Looks half as good to you
Although it may be humble
Although it may be small
But there is something there that satisfies
You guess its home that is all?
Now really it is not the house
Or a barn or yard I guess
That makes you so contented
Brings such happiness
So, I wonder what it is that makes a home so fair.
I have bout made up my mind:
It is because our parents are there.

Granny Rose adored poetry and dreamt of being a school's
principal. Rose loved being home with friends and family.
"No more death" Revelation 21:3,4.

A POEM A DAY

A poem a day
Should be my way
These poems I grow
I know that I know
Sometimes doubting
If what I see
They could say.
May at least
A poem a day
Be my way.

tanka i

betwixt birth and death
Lovelorns hope chaste hands to hold
all die some get borne
of the three struggles please say
which scare seems most difficult

Staying Near the Water

Staying near the water
There is a danger worth the bother.
Despite boundaries
Exuberance lends confidence.
As waves crash shores. Rage: brave and endless
Amazement in low ebbs, never enough victories
High tides, vile swells, gushing rocky reefs of grief
Content and alone as assets
Comfortable in the abstract
Excelling in awkward concepts
Fear of the reject.
"Poems are foolish," moan the vain and brutish
Can't be the only unprofitable stupid.
No time to read or make friends
Pouring over thoughts that ought line a litter box
Staying near the water.
'The water' is not my wife, sister, or daughter
It is truth needed in matter fluid
The source that emits knows keen and lucid
Impressive schemes, massive dreams—
Atrophy? No, my body gleans
What's important—Is not what's vital for me
Bartered memory of genes
Staying near the water
None go without the water
It's how we taste, see, and feel.
How intensely we recoil
Often will prove what's real
"What can be found in the ashes after the fire?"
Staying near the water.

haiku i

my health is my wealth
the body is the banker
see my deposit

Feet

Neglected poetry retells
Sorrow laden bare feet
Typically hidden not seen
Like a gifted child's elegy.
All have nooks and crannies
We wish no one to see
Toes burrow like beetles
At the sandy beach.
In tale feet dance in streets
Ultimate vulnerability
Is not offered willingly.
Embellished in fancy shoes
Feet touch ground
Simple and rude.
Imagine looking down on feet,
Feet doubly apt to condescend
Revealing: "you depend on feet."

spastic i

Am I a 'know it all' or is it all should know?
Wisdom acknowledges ears and nose.
Opinions too many, wasted argosy
What causes problems?
Sleep is best when we can't solve 'em
Hence *"requiesce in pace"*.

*" *requiesce in pace"* Latin literally 'rest in peace'.

Helpless

Victim or victory…lemme explain
We can verbal judo all day
But listen…
Once, I helped a man
(Think he had a broken hand)
Stand up from a fall
Support him like a wall
Onlooker's opened jaws
Hands in pockets and appalled
Maybe homeless, possibly diseased?
All he and I know; he is no longer on his knees.
I said, "he is like a baby's crawl
Helpless to all, how is it only sensed by the tall?"
Seeing dreams arrive
I, ta-ta waving
Like a Viking pyre fading.
Time after time, chance after chance
Prosperity and romance
Only earned a glance
This world has been a fast, sad torrent
Grim finding merit
Forgive me, I sound blew.
When I lunge my closed fist forth
There is only a smile
Yielding for sake of truth.

tanka ii

truth a comfort zone
shelved old souls are oft alone
plague maybe diseased
'aim' is not integrity
without truth we wilt on knees

JEWELS UNDER GLASS

Excuse me if I stare
My eye was arrested by the glare
Like jewels under glass,
I looked down as I pass.
My wandering mind means no harm
To promise you, I am charmed
Permit me, care I will take
As contact I wish to make
I will leave them as I found them
The self-consciousness will pass
They are like jewels,
Your jewels under glass.

haiku ii

her feet touch clay dirt
her understandings' give birth
her worth breaks new earth

BLASTS CONNECTIONS AND EXPLOSIONS

Blasts connections and explosions
Is there a word for 'good poisons'?
Killing negativity ending cold lonely
Blasts connections and explosions

Inner self: "Tc, can't recall, last time you…?
Blasts connections and explosions, whoa,
Love changes you!" blasts connections and explosions.

When the Universe creates something new,
Blasts connections and explosions?
When out of deep refreshing Blackness comes
Bursting Light. Blasts connections and explosions

When the Earth was formed; for Cynthia to walk on
Blasts connections and explosions
Beneath her feet is holy ground
Blasts connections and explosions

Ode to your abundance. A testament, to your power
Blasts connections and explosions
Each moment, what surrounds you? Each second
Each minute, each hour, blasts connections and explosions

MORNING GLORY

Week one: Bike ride to look around
Curious, my new hometown
Carthage, in its august bridge
Carthage, blooming and unassuming
Misanthropies unroll Lang Syne Auld
Demure and down-to-earth due equipoised
No pariah, HalleluJah! Eye to eye with ease
Denizens greet, wave, and smile
To guests on the street.
Looking down,
What is this I see?
Lissome, profound, and precariously petite.
Perhaps about a lattice
Though aimed and attached
Ideal a trestled walkway
Or borne a stone chimney
Securely adorning homes
Snug and copper domed
Ascend atoll gardens all discrete
Allied with weather-proof gnomes
Faithfully out of covetous reach.

Look! Morning glory
Verdant, with vines plied
In full bloom. After a warm
Tardy November night.
Incited by its mushrooming impudence,
I should like to say:
"Incipient and lush
On a public right of way
So Dainty! Do you think it prudent?

Across the sidewalk lay"
Zealous and aesthetic crisply glaring me:
"We don't choose our roots
These roots, they chose me!
Happily comply, assiduously proceed
Truth is not a curse and that I marquee!
You do what you can
Be what you will be.
The gas-lighting is egregious,
Yet Love Victoriously!
We cannot help,
Some on us want to step.
I burst from this cranny
Tomorrow all will see
The morning the glory
Belong to those like me."

Rare i

What does it take, When is?
How, if ever, swarthy viewed, viewed great?
Proxima Centauri on a canvas of swarthy
Then and only then, swarthy is not bleak
Even the unknowing notice swarthy victories.

A Prayer for The Sake of Etymology

Father Jehovah dear,
May we gladly reclaim words
Such as 'gaily' and its peers?
'Awful' is a lucid verb,
That has lost its reverential wear.
The phrase 'Auld Lang Syne'
Scots came to bear.
Characterizing the assurance of endurance,
An algorithm, your majesties prepared.
All strength belongs to you
And if a word is true
Your glory it declares.

*"Auld Lang Syne" the Scots language literally, 'old long since'

tanka iii

what we know of leaves
nearly half as much as trees
shed precious vapor
fed by photosynthesis
hues of nationalities

LEAVES (perhaps see Ezekiel 47:12)

Blithely dive in leaves
Trees shed their vapor
Helping us breathe
Curative properties, banquet varieties
Choice flora with untold leaves.
Humankind same many possibilities
Fruit, bark, and gene-specific parts
Abundance of life in leaves

spastic ii

Remember me as I wish
As that man who gives most but asks least
As that woman who nurtured a village,
Even if she didn't.
Dunbar said: *"We Wear the Mask."*
What behind the mask is hidden?
None of your business.

Brand New Black i (The Eve)

Black is contrast
Pure essence of depth
What is the limit? Black can
Say things life can't
When being gets too tough
If suicide persistently bluffs
Black says: "be that 'asshole'… dry those tears up."

Black, a state of mind
Unlikely to be taken light
Why don't meteors ruin earth?
The Black won't allow loveless blight
Ever been serious? Then passed black is stark
Black, home of other dimensions
Most fear some form of dark.

Though Black is your end
Black — the beginning, first thing — you did not see
When exiting the womb
Black is all we know
Before we debated morality
Most nursed pigmented areolae naturally

Black — Warmth that cannot be cooled
Black, burnt to a crisp yet Black is cold
The loving uses Black to scold
War is Black so is blood.

Woman is Black
Via her we are born
Black was Eve.

That is what her name means
"...She was to become the mother of everyone living."
Possible and nice to see light
Proving Black was done right.

*Perhaps see Genesis 3:20 [nwt]

haiku iii

I lost a new thought
such gems cannot be replaced
for want of a pen

keep a pen

Gone is a sketch, wisped in ether
Missed gem away forever
To my life was not tethered as
Vexing conscience and adversity.
Memories of memory
Flitting redeeming plea
A ruby, a notion that maybe,
God has not forgotten me
Sleeping in hunger waking in pain
Rare and positive, gone my day
Now its alleged, rendered in vain
Slipped and surrendered. Keep a pen.

Tie My Shoe

I learned your name and have not been able to
Not think about its gracinglyishseductiveness and you.
I have gold I have silver
Precious stones and metals, I have a few
I know sense, silence, and love
Sole intangible missing, is you.
When I was younger it was a rite
Something dearly from my heart to you.
I would look down… You would look down…
"Wait baby tie my shoe?"
I am only asking you to do
Something I am bending to do for you.
"Hold still baby I'm about to tie your shoe."

Truth Belated

Eff covid
We poets
Truth belated
Plandemic, we were sold it
What's next, we already over it.

Woman Water i

Nothing runs so deep
As the power that seeps.
If iron hones iron
Then tears sharpen cheeks
Time wastes in torrents
Can we measure 'intent'
(What units make sense)
Soft yet far from tame
Love stampedes and maims.
There is no hiding nor running
Only ducking, then dive in
Wished I could cope, pride is a dead end.
Neither Woman Water
Are killers to not dread
Two for our life,
For that, thank her twice.
Look how they burgeon
Precious like sturgeon
Prehistoric but no burden.

words

Words have color. Will I, enemy or brother?
Ashes regret burning bridges
Welcoming strenuous forgiveness
It's my choice, my words, my voice
Be the type who aids an adopted horse
Out of empathy speak. Those who kill, use words first.

Yester We

Remember we were kids
We'd make the simplest bids.
We'd giggle at the guileless
Plain joy with what's childish

Green holding grudges
Tears did exist.
Remember we were young?
Disappoint mutated
Our desires, dumb.
We sought friends who had nothing to offer
Threadbare we, yearning to not be a bother.

We hated to see fights.
Our dreams went further.
'Yester' thought we would be
Older versions of 'we.'
Am I who I thought I'd be?

tanka iv (perhaps see Song of Solomon 1:5,6)

You, rare and swarthy
So prettily found in space
Natural eyebrows
Like darkened slopes sit atop
Your pre-china sky-smooth face

Lissome

Lissome and petite
Nourishing and unique
Her stirrings sound so sweet.
Pound for pound
Tweet for tweet
Sparrows bludgeon earth
For a single seed.
Yet, her anger by comparison
Whisper's clement retreat.

I am Not Totally Visceral

Sexy is great.
Sex is best
When is valued
What is worth more
And not what's worth less?

haiku iv

love ain't Difficult
gimme gimme gimme ain't
difficult to me

spastic iii

This sadness is brewing
From where does it come?
Rather be braver but look what I'm doing.
To be mad, leaves me empty
At least anger is energy.
To be uncaring, is not to be forever
And not forever, is not me.

choices i (the pattern)

Truth is everything yet, nothing
If hearts lack to live it
Lavish opinions invent a 'critic'
Common questions brand the 'heretic'
Does truth have an equal?
Lies thrive best in truth's identity
Comedy is crucial
Amid five stages of grief
'It is what it is' convenience, blinded eyes seek
Is there One truth?
There is One source
Discreet voice, to each the choice.

"God offers to every mind its choice between truth and repose
Take which you please, you can never have both"-
Ralph Waldo Emerson

Red Chrysler Caravan

She drove red Chrysler caravan
Five-foot-four, her love spanned
She went to work when she had to
Played when she was mad too
You find a more loving man
My mission must and can
Jane, my Mother drove
Red Chrysler caravan.

Having a Conversation with Terry Herd (2008–2010 Sometime) About Why a Leaf Blower Was Not Effective with Cut Grass as the Object to Be Moved–I Used to Maintain His Yard from Time to Time

He said, "Obviously these offcuts were too heavy" —
I replied, "Well, its parings have no flight" —
He inferred; a leaf blower was useless.
I implied, flying grass is not right.

Ace Boon Koon

She is my Alfred, my Kato
She does not fight
She'd give k.o.
Calling when lost
Fleecy voice, worth all cost.
Scented touches excite
Simple meek delight
Needing her nights
Lest I am alone with frights.
If there was a cupid
She is it, kissing arrows
What else on, except her sexy though
Curved state, gripping her elbows
dreamlike to her ankles.

Gravity, Energy and Forever

Metals and stars fade
Though kelvin, suns have expiration dates
Who can hinge on water?
Water changes form
We can stand adversity
Then again, never lasts the storm.
So-called 'forever,' what really is it for?
Of known alien ideas, 'forever' has no peers
Watts rouses lights
Offering swell cheers
Of all the basics (not granted to understand)
'Forever' vexes hearts, not tangible hands
And this can be disappointing.
"Some choose to get high
In attempts to escape the minds potential
Some would rather die
Scorning life as a rental"
Failing to harness it
Yet, not harassed by it.
Just like voltage and its current
'Forever' has its unknown and its potent.
Gravity — friend nor foe
A short expedition into space
There is a different fall
Whereas on earth, one fears it all.

"The Sun does not have enough mass to explode as a supernova. Instead, it will exit the main sequence in approximately 5 billion years and start to turn into a red giant. As a red giant, the Sun will grow so large that it will engulf Mercury, Venus, and probably Earth. Even before it becomes a red giant, the luminosity of the Sun will have nearly doubled, and Earth will be hotter than Venus is today.

Once the core hydrogen is exhausted in 5.4 billion years, the Sun will expand into a subgiant phase and slowly double in size over about half a billion years. It will then expand more rapidly over about half a billion years until it is over two hundred times larger than today and a couple of thousand times more luminous. This then starts the red-giant-branch phase where the Sun will spend around a billion years and lose around a third of its mass." - a popular opinion.

Men Waiting

Two men were waiting in the DMV lobby. One a father. The other, a smug stranger who pretended to be interested as time seemed to waste while the unassuming child was being supported under the arms. With radiant countenance, the father, even if fleetingly, would tell every passerby everything he could about his growing child and himself. The humbug stranger seemed to have something in his nose, tough to loosen, as again the father gossiped of his improving child whom he believed, would soon talk and walk.

"What nonsense," the stranger grumbled. Too grand, he thought to himself. Kindled by the father's indomitable smile, the child did a motorboat sound with a summer toothed grin (some teeth are here, some are there). And for the umpteenth time, the child, though under the support of the father's hands, hit those chubby knees again and tears welled up, but the child was unable to cry; the father's hands were too soft, too warm, and too strong.

The stranger sighed an unqualified moan which was quickly bleached in the background. The father's main event was his child. The child gurgled, drooled, bumped its knees and let out a shriek. Now weary, the stranger's thoughts now amounted to audible slander of the driven but defenseless youngster. Just then, "Da," and for a lively moment a scuttling gait, before, "thud," went the child's knees.

"Ha, you've waited long and that's all that brat could do, was that worth all that boasting," the idle stranger taunted?

The untroubled dad ran to raise his child from the fall. The child was rapt in the father's tear-filled expression. The child's little frown mutated to mirror the father's shine. The father spun in circles. Rejoicing with laughter he cried out: "You did it. I knew you could do it. I witnessed it all!"

Sensing that good was done, dribbled puddled at the corners of the twirling child's mouth. Unexpected splashes of victory saliva dowsed the stranger's ceaseless pout. Wiping his mug, the stranger laid bare his bleak heart: "you call that walking and talking?"

"Yes," the father replied.

Jeremiah 31:20 "...is Ephraim not a precious son to me, a beloved child? For as often as I speak against him, I do remember him still. That is why my emotions are stirred for him. And I will surely have pity on him," declares Jehovah." (nwt)

If You Only Knew (everything is nowhere)

Why would I pause a spinning globe?
You are all I have in the world.
She is a sun when close to
Cautious of her refuge
Her pull claims my waking thought
When gone consumed by blinding dark
She is the cold unknown
Somehow I melt when close to.
My daydreams are barefoot stars
Spotting and increasing on you.

TeeKeyLA

Scent of TeeKeyLa, in the middle of the day
This boy gets annoyed *con agave* feted and parley
My work, my work, my work, slated to wait
Boho and rapt redolence betwixt the tips of the day.

*" con agave", Spanish literally 'with agave'

Changes (a true lst)

I ain't mad no more
Not confused not bored.
I ain't waiting no more
Found what I've looked for.

I am 'Tc' now!
A better Thomas
Changes. Our first
She believes in my promise.

Listening to her poetry
Lifts me to space
To levitate—no safety net
Trusting love face to face.
She says, I "make her brave"
She was that and more
I've just come to existence
Bunz' always been here before.

spastic iv

Becoming so nervous, words grow actions
Even libations won't calm frustrations.
Life be tired, honest, and under-esteemed
Would be easier to burn those dreams.
If Life cared what I thought
My opinion asked
When into the world I was brought.

tanka iv (perhaps see Jeremiah 13:23)

Tattoos on brown skin
Like adding stripes to zebras
What can be said that
Has not already been paid
Eminence of melanin

COWARD (perhaps see Revelation 21:8)

"A coward dies a million deaths"
This means it has had a million lives
A coward fears each fate
For now, the coward thrives
The coward does not know it is dead
Due to the *incredible* power of the lie.

*" *incredible*" Latin derived 'not credible'

Equivocate

Who's never said: "its
Okay," when it ain't—
"Good morning?"
For your reply we wait…
Truth may be disappointing
Huge decisions, can I capitulate?
Anything but, "Great!"
Would be to abnegate
We are well acquainted
With the equivocate
Not the choicest of best friends
Yet, the most cultured and virtuous of
This crusty earth's best men
Be it 'leading on,' pretense, or omission
Equivocation—Is next of kin.
Thanks to adages and maxims
We need not admit, it'd be a sin.
We hope our worth till morrow
Who don't have to beg and borrow?
With the dust this blood does blend
Does it bleed? Then it does end
Your love though, is it pure?
A good heart can make sure
Know your God, then no evil
"Our better angels" scheme like devils

This is "chess not checkers"
This monopoly eschews
Succumbing apologetics.
From an embryo to the grave
Certain truths I've had to stave

What infant isn't confident
Betided loins that begat
Furnishes the manse of tents.
Who but villains board jet planes,
Does not expect to see home again?
The old man vanguard intrepid
To a Future filled with
Fear of heights and the decrepit.
Call it 'paltry' sobriquet me 'petty'
Mealy-mouthed:
"Truths please comfort me?"
Sallying 'Beau Brummells'
Dare reveal what is real
Fully aware how its smarts kill.
Champions of chastity
Bloodletting heroes of honesty.
You are brave in the face of this knave,
Yet, you will depend on good friends
To temper candor and
Welcome you home again.

*"*Our Better Angels*" March 4th, 1861 A. Lincoln 1st inaugural address.

Flight from Orlando to San Juan

Voices from row forty-three
(Listening) I sit lonely
"mommy I cant reach"
Small, she stood on the seat
Jet plane ventilation inspired me.

haiku v

poor are like a tree
when there is real suffering
who is listening

Dios (perhaps see 1 Kings 8:27)

God is no man…never has been
Mortal depictions limit brilliance
The universe and the bleak — sheets
Where is what bed?
Happiness and love — food
What dreams' hopes in this head?
Killer and Savior
Drenched in the mantle
Marathon Warrior

*" *Dios*", Spanish literally "God"

Brand New Black ii

Twinkle away years blithest dots
Passing flames decadent sparks
Takes months to know
Are orbs alive that glow?
Funerals may take ages to see
Embalmed by Almighty Majesty
But the canvas. Brand new Black
Stars transient beholden guest
Class is black ever night Black is fresh
What would novae be
If humiliated by tacky light constantly?
Black privilege hard to leverage
Gathering—Black—Imperial genius
Famed galaxies enmeshed
Stranded in Black flash frozen gnats
Eons may retire, Black will never expire
Black growls: "foul," humbled Orion smiles
Brand new Black, backdrop and umpire.

BEGAT (thankfully)

Men of duty get legacy
Me confounded; he won't let it be
If I was one less, for me, he'd give his rest
A child's existence is the father's persistence
Long as dad lives
A seed's enemies contrive animus
Man of honor
A friend and father
Me, a hopeful product
A chance given to me
Your living blesses me

When my age, your grace upstaged
Indulgently lent a scapegrace your pay.
Romantic — your romance obeyed
In a romantic age.
A lie I may prove to be
How could you know I would be me?
Exuberance decrees
Because of seeds expectant
Fathers nearer eternity
A dad's unflinching love
Echos agape' from ago and above.

*When young, my raft drifted from a Lake Michigan beach. I could
barely see the shore
3-foot waves maybe more. My dad risked his. The float's rope, dad teeth
clinched. Forever thankful. Rage.

Algorithm

Simple numbers lie like servants
Algorithms assign laws instructions.
Deafening collective water disperse
Hidden recipes in the Universe
You must be cared plus be scared
Algorithms, blueprint flying lion bears,
Adjust neutron waves,
And score *Proxima Centauri's* final days.

*" *Proxima Centauri*" is the star nearest our sun.

Woman Water ii

You'd get wet, or drown
To her, your tears, femme rain
Woman, water, wonderment, no bane
No pain if lost face is no shame.
Instinct trumps "No"
Forfeit that pride for it is all show
Woman water — necessity no foe.
Woman water — killers, thankless,
Restless, and natural blue when tankless.
Incessantly sorry, yet incredibly unforgiving
My life will change if I continue living.
Water's sole effect is when soothingly wet —
Could be true, but don't forget
Hydro-thermal phenomena to arid glacial effects.
Woman, the resource; pure liquid a marvel
Dryness is neglect, less moist let life unravel
Lifeblood of society, is it all pre-Adam?
Water, I empathize to its trace elements
Suffer to decipher woman's raw affects.

We (the same)

May be of different 'colors'?
But the borders that rut us
Are the knives that cut us
Our brotherhood, interrupted
The same Kalashnikovs gut us

three words (ptsd)

Initially one knee
Things change swiftly
Begging for peace
Dirt in eyes
Making me cry
At three words
Shelling sleepless sigh
Dishes hit floors
Child go hide
Working plus hours
Ready to die
'I love you'
Did my best
Who can deny?

Soon

Studying 'Woman Water'
Sadness is slaughtered
Promised healing lifts sorrow invalid
I wonder, "why is the truth so torrid?"
Wanting to be happy
Coveting 'nappy'
Truth, a mother, who won't have
Truth, a father, backsliding, don't dab
So goes the fun or so it seems
From where come the notion 'sweet dreams'
Emotion is clay soon to be redefined
Adages and maxims will be rediscovered,
As if from behind.

spastic v

Loneliness was sexy — is anyone lonely
Lonely may melancholy, suddenly humble
No, then maybe sexy lured them into trouble
For the bold, humble is a strange expression
Only and lonely do a rhyming impression
Strange, how sad became that way
Company was wrong so sexy slithers away.

Sexy (perhaps listen to 'Second Time Around' by Luther Vandross)

Solo & sexy sitting in the sun
Away from the trouble of fun
Sexy is a time, everyone gets but two:
A chance to do their best and a choice to rise anew.

Mr. Meads

Dear Mr. Ross Meads,   March 1, 2011

I would like to congratulate you for having an integral share in an educational program that is growing in fame. Crossroads Charter Academy of Big Rapids, Michigan is the program to beat. The Cougars are a highly contending program that is drawing much attention for sports and academics.

The sports are doing so well, there is an enviable following wherever the Cougars compete. Money is tight in these times so that is something to be proud of. I am immensely proud of my nephew Jalen Carter.

My nephew and his peers leave me impressed. For what I understand your young people are driven, courteous, and concerned about others. This is not an accident. They are getting encouragement for good behavior. I thank you for your part. As a school bus driver, at times I observe students and how they react to their environment.

Most recently Crossroads' men's varsity came to play basketball at Baldwin High School. I enjoyed the smiling faces and happiness the game was offering to all. Cougar support did not fail to show up. Cougars' fanbase may have been more plentiful than Panthers'?

As the event progressed, players and fans became emotive. Joy left the young men like helium leave balloons. The student players began to resemble gladiators. An apoplectic Cougar's fan shouted, "SIT DOWN," to a ruminating Panthers' coach.

Cougars had it under control since tip off. Sometimes poor sportsmanship can be found in the dominant. Your young men took a fine victory. Confident and focused to the end. Still, I cannot set aside the importance of the fans' impact on the team. The young men have fine lives ahead of them and things will turn out well for us all without making them feel as if they must be out for blood. I cannot deny them the right to play hard, but is there anything we can do to help guard against being sore winners?

Right now, the scales are tipped in our favor due to abundant talent, dedication, and support of some well appreciated fans. With all due respect and love for my nephew Jalen Harvey Alexander Carter, I write this letter. And as a delighted devotee, "GO COUGARS!"

Sincerely,

Thomas H. Carter

Kissing in the Kitchen

Chance mid-day passing
Your dizzy friends, out-front waiting
Lunch break running late
Tonight? Don't have the patience
My weakness — you, in that apron
Wasn't supposed to happen
My fingers, your scalp in
Squishy hips sated grasping
Tongues twining, lips vining
Trading vices, I mess Your hair
Cars honking, you must not care
In romance we drowning
Unsung bosses calling.
Afternoon delighting.

Joe Stout

We met the day
I returned a Budget truck
You became a friend of good *luck*.
Akin, dopamine, and brain waves
Debates lasting months of days
For the ages you remain.

* "'Luck' is opportunity that you are ready for." — Denzel Washington

Idlewild, Michigan i (2009 State of Mind)

We bleed parallel with greed
"Buy from me" peddlers plead.
The only multiplying one gets
Is increasing time spent
When is the last time I've been
This long away from hearth from kids?
Good buildings gone to seed
Grass on the roofs
Weed filled gutter veins
Limbs plummet on cherished gazeboes
Will it be discovered?
Next season we will see.

haiku vi

black firsts human births
Noah sires Ham at the crux
same diverse hued dirts

an old opinion on love

bold for no reason
flesh can humble stone
unsubtle and blunt
impartial and lifting pale heavy hope
Love will not settle for less, feeding off sincere
Love cares if I am gone. Love cares if I am here.

Bursting Comet–to Ashley (July 4th, 2020)

I saw a bursting star
Then appeared your hair
Springy and shining
Glowing everywhere
That day I met you,
Wow a sunbeam.
For the honesty in your face
I drove one thousand miles.
The peace in you
Makes those who love you smile.

MEPHIBOSHETH FROM LODEBAR
(perhaps see 2nd Samuel 19:24-30)

Languid but wise
Tested and tried
He said "keep it all"
My soul is supplied
The anointed is safe
This servant is satisfied.

Righteousness by Violence

Such is violence
Knows no color
Respects no fence
Boundaries merely
Mistaken intelligence.
Moral superiority begets
Righteousness by violence.

smile

You left something…
This smile on my face,
An incipient sign of humanity.
The best of me, I have felt all day.
It is yours to leave behind,
Or it is yours to take
I will be remiss, till from you I know
How you left this smile on my face.

That's You—to Nikki
(Her Paintings Took Me to Salvador Dali's World)

A medley that's you
Confuse me with delight
Am I happy or gleeful?
Joyful with youthful intent
Yes, you can
Without consent
Make me smile
Make me wonder
You were that dimple
Intense and simple.

Sarah

Time has come
To remember her
Kindergarten or shortly before
My best friend Sarah and I
Played, knees on floor
Invented, *plu-splendid*
Ready to live
Sarah a taker
Eager to give
She lived as I dream
Followed my games
When others were around
Sarah went, later was found
Shy and quiet to the world
Sarah made no trouble
We were always clean
Never a scheme
Good together
Gaucho and leather.

*" Plu-Splendid", self-coined verb or adjective, literally 'passed perfect'.
**"gaucho" South American cowboy of the pampas, known to have a
remarkably close bond with his pony.

THE BURDEN IS NOT UNIQUE

Knowledge boons night
Conviction revives a twilight bright.
Hope for hope when there is no control
This day would come, long ago foretold.
Weakened once wrought institutions
Hemorrhaging moralities
'Getting by' wilting unions
What remains of poor municipalities?
Hope for hope and test the ropes
When stooped low, not assuredly tall
Victors stand, victims fall.
Hope is not all, yet, has a certain draw
Must be good cause
Why for so many is rescue on pause?
Is it that 'luck' has not deemed us 'fit'?
Hope—an educated subject
Luck—a breeze, a befuddled suspect
Luck—cheap material, life on it cannot expect
Luck—respires unhappy, fickle and brief
Luck—will not move you to rise to your feet
As an indebted man, fights yet ahead
Tape of will wraps hands
Hope, (just in case) helmet to the head
Opinions and rights, hollow as the flesh's stem
Who issues attitudes?
Must be something I choose
Jehovah arranges paths that cannot lose

Idlewild, Michigan ii (new beginnings)

If the country is my father
And the city my mother
Then yes, heavenly Sovereign
I have been orphaned and aborted.
With your promise grant through service
Peaceful and abiding solace.
Awaken me, your servant —
Requests another chance.

Little Lotus Blossom

Little lotus blossom
Afraid to see the sun
Proxima Centauri charm
You are light and distant
How can the sun harm?
Your envy is a virtue
Bright copper arms.

Puerto Rican Parking Lot Pigeon

I said: "Move, move pigeon
Negra pollo estupido
Move, or your life lose,
Move for the love of good."
I listened: "O' me, I am a dove."
Strutting in the road

*" *Negra pollo estupido*" Spanish literally 'black (feminine) chicken stupid'

some her some more

Any star will singe you,
Get close enough
Any bull will toss you,
Promise, he is rough enough
Any vehicle takes you to point 'b'.
Why not believe
Her love and her more
Will not move a mountain
Or completely change a world

Alive

Victim or victory—choose
Butt-naked or clothed, can't wear both
Casket filled with me empty of hope
Its shrewd I be smoked
Pass my finest suit
To the next young poke

With haste and must
Haters wish we die penniless
Lowered and left to rust
Be rich in love
Before claimed by the dust

While living, fascinated with biology
At war times, ready for battle consistently
When a friend needed
Opportunities led to sincerity

Best is over, don't feel bad
Regrets few, laughed more than sad
Show your dreams you are more real
Time is a test, when it is passed
Say "Thank you, I had the choice to feel"

Mine

Why o' why
Becoming the
Object of my astonishment.

Why o' why
When you are at work
I have business too
I sit and watch the clouds

On your smile
My victories march
Don't often see the likes of me, do ya?
Thinking of you, I holler, "*Hallelujah!*"

* "*Hallelujah*" Greek literally "Hail Jah" shortened form of "Jehovah"
("JHVH") transliterated Hebrew "YHWH"

choices ii

Choices reach grave doses
If 'actuality' came full strength
No other options but to do it!
Seldom not diluted
If censors have opinion
Fact is thinned excuses
If imperfection is all we have,
What is common sense and improvement?
Rank of rights used rope-like
Fog of war, if, as, and by
'Arbiters' Elegantea'
(a spurious parody of Christ —
if peace were black
these would not have
enough to call it 'a night')
May strangle grandma.
Exploiting principle like a wish
Justice be damned
Next generation impoverished
Choices will always be the same
Those with power will never change.

*" Arbiter Elegantea" Latin literally 'Judge of Elegance'

Like Electricity

"Like," is Life's ubiquity
Life shares electricity
Every day is circuitry
Future bonding history
I love your thread and memories
There will never be enough
Time around. So, for now,
I wire my knee: "connect her ground."

They Were Known as 'Savages'
(perhaps see Genesis 9:27)

Shaping and wandering earth
Leagues of Japheth through great feats
Some standing, others miry heaps.
Who lunges first?
Wrestling Siberia's endless
Extinct memories blurred people
No charter, just icy water.
Tired woman, bent-over elder,
Suckling, and *doula* in tow
Where our next sun rises…
Do not ask, just go!
Land bridge crosses purpose and mission,
Hunt and be hunted
The only condition.
Over frozen soil
Masters of self survivors' toil
Working to eat slightest spoils
How many souls did 'enduring' cost?
Insurance and vaccinations a hype a loss
Broad and gritty visions — created nations
Where is the credit for savvy navigation?
Pioneering and vanished civilizations.

*" *Doula*" Greek, literally 'female slave' or 'woman who
serves'

Natural Accountability

Jehovah crafts alphas easily
Sequence fit for legacy
Yet men lust fanning sympathy
Masculine becoming flimsy
Challenging her for femininity.
Jehovah shakes his head inaudibly
Men then seek
From other men, authority.

If You Point Your Heart at Me

Don't you dare!
Just because, I can't help but stare
Don't you pull it out
You are what this is about
Until you are ready to use
9mm and 38 SIGs just tools
Different from my dream-woman's heart with rules.
Don't be fooled; are you sure?
You know — I am who misses you more.
Open to me
I will take it seriously
You show me to the family
I will encourage them
And try to make them need Tc
You will not want to share me
Always making sure you
Have an escape route
I keep a flak vest.
Tc protector of your chest
You've never met any similar to me
None are comparable to you
(except poetry)
I will share my heart with you
If you point your heart at me.

tanka vi

if the aim is friends
black sunflower bird feeder
want to help mankind
keen need for avid readers
people are worth toiling for

LUNA (perhaps see Psalms 89:37)

Luna, your father the light
The reflection your mother
Luna's dust praises bright
Luna 'the witness' waxing delight
Keenly scheduled nights
Earthlings seek apartheid and fright
Imperfection...your worse betrayer
Black rainbow swarthy and right
Luna's halo reigns, waning helpless sleep tight.

*" Luna" Latin Literally 'Moon'

Grok

Anxious lackey crab-climbing
Sneakily, female emulating
"To win her approval — is all to me?"
Synthetic leaders look to her for decency
Monetized womb unhinges validity
She will give in naturally
Standards of beauty seize her femininity.
Misuse of life-saving maxims
Cleverly horded metals guessing then fixing values
Encouraging exclusion, oligarchs award libations
Disenfranchisement an option, not a limitation
Grok mythology, 'gods' return flattery
Stoops peak at controlling men
Culling humans shape human being
There is stop-gap gain in believing
A preeminent sentient is not seeing.

*"*Grok*" to understand intuitively or by empathy
A word coined by author Robert Heinlein (1907-1988). 'Stanger in a
Strange Land' (1961)

Certificate of Vaccine I.D.

Eve framed the snake
Aids, HIV, and 80's blamed the ape
C.o.v.i.d. entraps the bat
Placed in our custodies
Voiceless animals under constant subtle
Attack deceitful husbandry
Means honorable name of snakes and apes
Pale to limitless human savagery.

*Perhaps see Genesis 3:13

haiku vii

key hints make haikus
fused pith with short-spaced tools
these may quicken truth

Regrets...I Clean

'Hope', a rare form of neglect
Accept, don't ignore it
To status clout, only the trivial is important
Something went wrong, invented was hope
Unwillingness mutated, began a need to cope.
Who has ever faked insanity,
Belongs with King David
Of ancient survival history.
Like a Figure '8,' good linking evil
What seems to be the middle
Simply — an opinion that squiggles
Messes make me smile
Regrets, I clean!
Best way to avoid sting
Make sure that bridge
Is burnt to a crisp
Regrets, I clean, give me the assignment
Ties made stronger with true forgiveness.

Mikayla (Pleasant Shade, Tennessee post office)

Sensibilities of society
Up Saturday dawning
When men feel most sorry
A woman is busy
Not waiting, but simply…
Most beautiful I've seen all morning.
En route peeked grass and trees,
On the forest floor there was a leaf.
None of these stopped
What they were doing to look at me.
Parcel — not even ready,
A hurried spring bloom
Mikayla accepted patiently.

How to Love Her (unsolicited advice to Aaron)

Your queen she is becoming
May she weigh the thirst for weaving
Symphonic is her breathing
Nice to hear her every night
Weather against impulsive leaving
Some rain is growing pangs
See her hands, skin, and feet
We are not yet replete
Know her modesty and toes
This is romance
Make the most.

spastic vi

Spoofing elegies
Or do elegies spoof me?
One or the other is vain proof.
More complexity than
Piano keys, these elegies
Act as heart strings
A lethal instrument I do not 'play.'
So, I goof with my pen
In place of mandarin proverbs, I cannot say.

Shady Love on Green Mountain (2019)

Shady on green mountain 2019
This is a cool spring
Brook, in the back babbling
Barely above eighty
This long into May?
Love seems visual
Surface and congenial
Love is a thing often pitiable
Our emotions play a part
Like the brook in the back murmuring
Mostly it is the eyes
That zeal and do the bullying.

tanka vii

Do you want children
Still how can pretty help them
Giving you what you
Need somehow leaves me wanting
Greed spawned new seeds is haunting

Love Miss Takes

We made a lot of mistakes
Making us the most of lovers
One poet named Miss Womack said
You can't make one without lots of the other.

My Love Is Like Your Back

I love like your spine
Well-rounded with signs
You will sigh thrilled
When gripped by the hips
Finessed womb filled

The dip in your back
Is deep as is tall
My love is the cliff
Yoke my rhyme and never fall

My arms are veils twisting vines
Craving your body that
Copiously awash for mine.
Back of your head in my palm
All connecting surfaces soft.

My love is your lips
Juicy, ripe, and yielding pain
But pastel as black rainbow silk
Serenading sweeter midnight rain.

Sunny to shadowy
My love, indulgently replete
Like her new undercut
To the smooth soles of her feet.

She Was Born in a Storm (goodbye again, hard to keep her)

Fearlessly, she made him fearless
(Because he was sorry)
Failing at my best
Good intent never gives rest.
Never committed, barely situated
Now she is on her way, ready to change.
From now on, every single day.
She is dangerous. Why?
Cause for her, someone is ready to die
It is simple to see
If she is accosted, someone will bleed
Even if it is only me
So, call her a killer
She was born in a storm
From a sea of blissful peace, she was torn.

spastic vii (sterile truth)

Dexterity of thought
Belong to the content
Malpractice is egregious
To an ungodly extent.
Sterile truth an
Eleven roofed house
No rain may get in
But what air or prayer gets out?

Sacrificing Sick

Often accused me of ailing
My sacrifice I'm questioning
Me "bi-polar?" But high functioning
My focus monies optioning
Remember times, I wished I were dead?
Mozambique was her dream
Ask her, "who flew you to the motherland?"
From the way she acts,
I learned Eve was 'black'.
Eager to prove
She was my water, we became fluid
And moved. Thinking she needed proof
Really, seeking to seclude, I was, "too close to my family."
What villain merits such torturing?
Loving my wife as best I could
I got my sick friend back, by sacrificing and leaving her.

Lullaby Minds

Rap a lullaby
Many woke to after
Chips & dip and negligence
Paid our own soul narcotic
Salvaged innocence
We were drugs of chicanery
Done getting high
80's what a party
Either lost our minds or died.

Sorry

'Hope' a rusted gun
Not a natural frame of mind
'Hope' and 'sorry'
Sounds right some time
Last one sorry for me is me
Sorry is for those better than me
Sorry is sorry needs
Sorry is a strong man seeking to please
Sorry is a child, who has lost his hope
Sorry is a... sorry is unable
Unwilling to cope...

tanka viii

The winds never stop
Winds do not billow in vain
Winds move us onward
Closer to humility
With lack of love our sole tool

WINDS (perhaps see Revelation 7:1-3)

Winds do not blow in vain or futility
Winds move us
Closer to the day of humility.
We arrived in this world exposed and unclothed
Our only tools — helplessness and love.

'Flower'

They call me 'flower'
Not because they are congenial
But because of sugar water
Horror when I am late
Tiny spite darting terror
With *iridescent* power, o' they buzz my tower
With horned-face belligerents
Pummel one another
'Hummer' by misnomer
Thunderbirds threats and wonder
How many flaps
Do wing beats take?
(That split one *second*, but look fake)
To seek a northern Summer.

*" iridescent" due to a phenomenon called 'iridescence' the black throat of the male ruby- throated hummingbird glistens like a ruby when exposed to sunlight.

** a second can be split indefinitely.

Contrary

Cyclothymia and its abject rain dance
Imperious Atlantic's demoralizing cadence
Thorn and millstone,
Don't get along.
Is 'happy' in itchy burlap hammocks?
Out of rhythm and emotional violence.
Living false the worst menace:

face is lite
guise is bright
reputation a lie
promises virtuous
results are excresence
semblance, oh yes envious
implying pious symbiosis
transparent airs whose nature is atrotious

Pain is pending when her eyes are blinking
Come with it suspicions without endings
Since was made a conjugal pact
How do I take my word back?
There it comes
Millstones and thorns
Here it goes
Cycles versus the currents
No repose.

Unreal (interstellar love search)

Breathe…come far to find you…
I've traversed the black and space
Self-centered novae, oxygen waste

Galactic lashes, material worm hole
Celestial eyes, unavailable emotional
Endless taking as Saturn's seldom giving
Romanceless circles meaning lost
Time in unworthy dimensions

Justified. Finally, here with you
Is like a rainbow in a place
Where hue has no relevance.

Rare ii (knowledge love black: rare yet everywhere)

Heavens are black, think a bit
Why God chose to dwell in it?
Love, universal element
Yet only earth prove love exists.
Where was love before this rare?
Love and black are everywhere
Afore mirrors all were bare
Symbolically black loathed as lack.
'The tetragram' (YHWH) asked the man,
"Who told you that you were naked (Genesis 3:11)?"
Eve black pilot mom
Love rare dulled pre-dawn.
'Nekkid' gifted
Fig leaf traded
Quitted is benign and lucid
Condemning children to the dirt
Adam presumes God perverse
If we were light, we did not know
Dark a force, backs Gregor Mendel
Now black seen through a window
Prim and Privilege wish 'it' not join in
We admire (even naming) distant dancing constellation
While insulting the bliss ballerinas' twinkle in.
Betting we are safe because cold dark
We repelled, as if black were afraid of stark?

Want to Try Something New

Most weekends my father drove to Woodland Park, often taking my brother Lawrence and me with him. Woodland Park has a rich history with working class residents. Woodland Park is in northern Newaygo County Michigan. This time was special. We would always prepare for anything because there was so much to do 'Up North': ride horses, fishing, basketball, target practice, swimming. We had friends there and family would come from places far away to vacation. To boys like us there was no chance to be bored in Woodland Park. Lawrence and I were on the same page. Whatever Lawrence wanted to do; I was ready.

Leaving Kalamazoo, we headed north on U.S. 131 business loop. Whitney Houston and Journey played softly above a comfortable quiet between us.

"see," my Dad said suddenly, "see, we did not do things like that when we were young."

"what you mean," I asked?

When exiting the village, we witnessed children playing in the streets, some nearly being hit by cars. We could see the police reprimanding some; others were smoking! These were not unusual scenes. Lawrence and I knew this type of stuff was not our style. Lawrence defended them anyway: "ain't nothin else to do", he said. I knew my father would have a response to that.

"boy!", my dad exclaimed, and then he started to recall things he did in summertime as a youth. Keep in mind, my father was raised in the woods of northern Michigan, which was a different cultural experience from the burg of Kalamazoo where we grew up.

Despite himself, my father's recollections were working. "Want to try something new? What about hunting?"

"hunting?" I gasped, I thought hunting had to be done strictly in autumn.

"man listen, we hunted something year around," my father said, "...and summer is bullfrog time."

"camping out all we needed was a .22 rifle, or pellet gun, skillet, flour, knife and campfire," dad said. Then, "shoot the bullfrog, cut off the back legs, skin 'em, flour dip 'em and drop 'em in hot grease. Eat 'em however you want: hot sauce, ketchup, or fresh off the fire."

The first two hours of our drive, he told us stories, preached firearm safety, talked of shooting tragedies, and recited poems he had written of his childhood. I treasure my dad's 'beens' and 'ustas'. Lawrence and I were new to frog hunting, we asked many questions. Finally, we needed to know one thing further:

"where do we find those bullfrogs?"

"Staying near the water," Dad said simply.

It was hard to believe. Such an impressive meal inhabits virtually any organic structure of water's edge. As we neared Woodland Park, we readied our gear. Bumping the ceiling simultaneously we caught the same gleam in each other's eyes.

"Lawrence, you got enough ammo?" I asked.

"yeah, how about you?" he countered dutifully.

"yep. knife, flashlight?" I asked

"got 'em" he said.

Our equipment checks complete, my brother the general, gave the final instructions: "be quiet when we approach the waters."

"hey," dad said, snapping us out of our reverie, "meet me back at the park."

When my dad's van doors opened, two *euxenite* males jumped out like Sioux braves about to count coup. Excited and silent. Invigorated by the forest air we were good to go.

"shh... I see one," Lawrence whispered. "Pichew," went the sound of my brother's air gun. When we learned it took more than one pellet to treat or disable our prey, we instituted the "firing squad". That is what we would say when either of us spotted a bullfrog. The other would come running to assist. "On the count of three," a pellet volley followed. We must have bagged at least fifteen frogs (thirty legs) that first night. After we felt we had exhausted the creeks supply of croakers, we called it a night. But there were thousands more. Reluctant to leave, but sated, we knew we would be back to-morrow. When we finally rendezvoused with our dad, not a single detail was left unshared. Dad smiled through it all.

Roughed up and mosquito bitten, we dressed our catch, separating the bullfrog legs from their riddled bodies and putting the delicacy on ice. We had decided a second haul (the next night) would make them more of a meal. On our way down state my dad asked, "did you have fun?"

*"*Euxenite*" brownish black mineral with a metallic luster. Greek etymology "friendly to strangers, hospitable" in allusion to the rare elements it contains.

tanka ix

gimme treats esteem
sigh when our pay simplified
YHWH did not cry
"get up save us now we tired"
His servants objectified

Untitled (she is a spaceship)

I am black, vast blackness.
You — the vessel
Closing my distants
My smiles — quicker
Language — bolder
Goals — easier to vision
My heart and mind
Enter quantum unison

Persimmon

Small, darkened, hid in hearts of grass
Looking down as I pass
Like *"jewels under glass"*
Persimmon season
November narrow and fast
Southern delicacy
Chance at long last
Unmistakable texture
Rich memories of being penniless
Waking first is squirrels
On our heels, autumn chill unfurls.
Fruit drops like degrees
Eating too soon will bitter your teeth.
No more leaves — high in trees
Waits 'My Persimmon' to be
Patient as granny, gravity loves me
She will not be rushed — she will be she
She is the beautiful Persimmon tree.

On My Fingers (turquoise)

Tracing your hue
Turquoise and lovely
Sliding above me
By your touching
Roughed stones smoothed
Like sand you slip
My fingers through
Water seek her form
Hair hands taste
Inside her violence storm
Verse explains her face
High cheeks quote nape
Stir her dimple her quakes
It is a wonder I am here
Never have I dreamt more clear

Woman Water iii

"Thank you for having my infant,"
Water, scorned as pesky liquid
Woman as man's archenemy
When mankind gets dry and solo
From where will we get more?
A threat — real and great
Our world — these influences shape
Wars take needs for granted sake
Common miracles opened wombs opened earth
Give them breadth give them birth
Offered less... a future will slurp
Sap of goodness
Lush border shores washed away.
The nod to life — these authorize, and death deny supply
Monsoon inundation — same toll and boon menstruation
Both grin and glisten, men die for the powers listen
Can a true giver be too needy?
Woman water — my ample desire. Does that make one
greedy?
To make fertile takes no work
What guile? — unassuming innate worth
Makes no difference — without these we die poor
Rejected murky impure
What one-man trashes, another works for
Violence never spared
Woman water crucial as air.

Raise me up yes, they can raise me
Help me heal me baptize and bathe me
Touch me touch me how only you can touch me
You consume and then delude me

Make me feel as if I am thee
Religious virtue hath no integrity
If in thy worship, thou art scanty (selah).

Moisten away the bleak, manhood at times unsavory
Sparkling femininity, rare, please and plenty
Show my son respect me
Woman helps cope, our race itches a self-destruct
House of life and preternatural fluid
Nurture and impelled to do it
Displacing mountains and whole nations
In your abundance or in your vacance
Woman, water, and truth must not be stilled
Is it that homogeneous beauty kills,
Or is depth where hell thrills?
"She was too this...too that"
The affidavit is where you will find it.
Rare men fight necessary war
Prosperity nevermore
Gone is peace water and woman
With less value, damaged cistern
Where can these smile undisturbed?
Crumbling water our very nature unnerved
Takes a spiritual man with intent
To say, "no!" — disdain strangling with plastics for profit.
Lack of priority and home
Same as spit
Children, garden — warped growth in it
Poverty, are these isolate frays?
The same loss the same tribulation
Our woman our water isn't a sacred occasion?
Death claims us when these are tainted
Do not hoard only need water deserves right

Leave her alone if she is no treat
End lies, same criminals as faithless harsh chemicals
Corrupt beauty standards dam the flow
If they love us, which they do,
These will cycle and dawn our new!
Protect then console
Within the pair reprieve the soul.

*Thinking of Ziauddin (father) & Malala Yousafzai (daughter) and our disintegrating/rotting relationship with water.

** "*Selah*"- "Technical term for music... found in Psalms and Habakkuk... pause {3 to 10 seconds} in the singing or music, for silent meditation to make the sentiment just expressed stand out. The Greek Septuagint rendering is diapsalma, defined as "musical interlude."- nwt

She... je ne sais quoi

Vengeance is ending
Wastes time hiring henchmen
With her voice she does the killing
Making life, her purpose her mission
Grok her soft her love
Her willing was that link that was missing
Seems why God sent a dove

* *"je ne sais quoi"* French literally "I don't know what"

How This Works

If you like it, I love it
If you love it, I love to love it
If you are not sure I'm here to assure you
Giving me mine
Guarantees your value and time.

haiku viii

keen stoic insight
transcends arranged religion
pals with common sense

All I Have is Yours

Scent sweat hair
On the pillow there
Gone is her touch
Hurts to miss her this much

Silken fading face
Reminiscent of space
Gone black and everywhere
Evoking her in my hands fails... just air

She is here and there it's clear
What I want she takes away
What was mine, leaving thru doors
Yes, all I have is yours.

tanka x

need food though evil
caged hater and raged neighbor
fussy stomach's brains
dear dental's health in peril
sly heart goads me more junk please

ODE OF JUNE

I finished this tonight
Thinking out of thin air:
"Jane and Larry 'turned up' for me?"
Enfant terrible.

* I'm a March baby
**" *Enfant Terrible*", French, literally 'terrible child'

end